I Still Know What I Know

Gail Alexander

I Still Know What I Know

copyright ©2019 by IbbiLane Press

All rights reserved. No part of this book may be reproduced or utilized in any form or by any means, electronic or mechanical, including photocopying , recording, or by any information storage and retrieval systems, without permission in writing from the publisher.

ISBN/SKU:9780578455730
ISBN Complete:978-0-578-45573-0

Dedication:

First, I would like to dedicate this book to my parents. It is through their deaths that I have learned the greatest lessons about life.

To my uncle for being who he is. He has had more of an impact on my life than he will ever know.

To my brother, my hope is that one day this will all make sense.

I would like to also dedicate this book to all of the amazing human beings who have shown up in my life, who have supported, loved and helped me through some of the most difficult times of my life. I would also like to thank them for all the fun and laughter.

I have had two therapists over the years who have each changed the course of my life. One when I was younger who literally saved my life and saw me for me when no one else did. The second one who helped me through my parent's transitions and showed me that just creating a sacred space for someone can sometimes be just what they need. Both listened and encouraged me and I am forever grateful. Both always saw and nurtured my gifts even when I did not. Thank you does not seem like enough. You will both have my eternal gratitude.

To my colleagues for letting me be me, while sometimes taking a bit of a different path and also trusting in me.

To all my teachers thank you for the lessons.

To my publisher thank you for always believing in me and trusting my vision even when I did not always see it clearly.

To my editor, thank you for making me sound good.

Table of Contents

Introduction

Section One:
    Narrative

Section Two: The Science Fiction Moments of My Life
    Experiences with Dolphins
    Abduction
    The Priestesses of Isis
    Healing
    Healing Classes
    Bilocating
    Ice Beings
    Control Panel & Science Fiction Moments
    Being a Medium
    Mandalas

Section Three: Channelings, Messages to Humanity
    Prayer
    Connection
    To The World
    Dear Ones
    To Humanity
    Jesus Message
    Kuan Yin Message
    Mother Mary Message
    Gaia Earth Mother Message

Section Four: Meditations
    The Blue Flame Meditation

The Healing Light Meditation
The Golden Christos Light Meditation

Epilogue

Introduction:

I had been trying to figure out what direction this book was going to take. I have discovered that part of my process is to give up trying to control and just let it pop in. Depending on the information I am receiving it takes a different amount of time. I refer to this process as getting or being downloaded. I compare it to when a computer gets an update to its software. I get updates, information, and codes to help humanity continue to evolve.

In writing this book, I decided to just trust that it would make sense by the time I was done. Then it clicked in, this book was going to follow a similar format as the first book: I Don't Know How I Know. . . I Just Know. I am going to include some of my science fiction or woo woo moments as I like to call them, channelings, and meditations. I am going to include a mandala for each section to hold the frequency and vibration for that section.

One of the things you will quickly ascertain from me is that I am a straight shooter and I am not afraid to put things out there. So as I said in book one, buckle up. It is going to be a bumpy and interesting ride.

Section One:
Narrative

Narrative:

I have struggled with being an empath my whole life. I was particularly empathic around pain and illness and I found this really hard to reconcile. I would see, feel, and know how people were receiving the messages and what their physiological and emotional responses to the messages were. I had no idea what to do with this information. I did not have any one to talk to about any of the things that were happening to me. I felt so alone and out of place. I never fit in and that is all I really wanted. I just wanted to be normal and I was far from it. My solution: shut it all off. Albeit, in retrospect, this was not the healthiest choice. However, it did work for a period of time. I stopped getting messages and I stopped paying attention to my guides.

Over the years as my gifts and abilities have come back. I have had to make adjustments with how I interact with people and what I chose to share and what I keep to myself. This has posed a dilemma. When people find out that I am intuitive, a medium, or medical intuitive, they want to ask me questions all the time. I have found my gifts to be hard to manage at times because of this. It is hard to be around people and get so much information even when you are not trying to receive any.

One of the things that was particularly hard for me in the beginning when I did readings and everyone would cry. This was very hard for me to understand and be witness too, as it has never my intention to hurt anyone or cause anyone pain. It took me a long time to realize the tears are a release. As I have gotten older I have learned to see this as a gift. Being able to connect to people on a soul level is a profound experience. We all want to feel connected, we all want to feel seen and that we matter. This is often times what my readings do. I now feel fortunate and blessed that I get to do what I do. I have let go of the fear and come from a place of love and light. I am not responsible for how people take in the information. My part is to just be as clear as I can to have the information come through as unfiltered as possible.

At a young age I knew that being there for people was important and I knew that having a compassionate and open heart was imperative. Just being present with someone can make all the difference in the world even if no verbal communication happens. I had forgotten this for a long time because I was so busy trying to accomplish things and build a career that I forgot to just be.

I have tried to keep my childlike joy, wonder and curiosity about the world and my fellow human beings. I have been called a dreamer. I believe miracles can happen. I have seen what can happen when you trust, have faith and are able to stay in the present and let go of an outcome. I choose to see the world as a place of possibilities and miracles, not limitations and pain.

Perception of how you see the world is a choice. We all have a choice of how we live, what we say, what we believe, and how we want to be as a human being. We are called human *beings* for a reason. It is about being. Being mindful, being present being grateful, and having a sense of faith.

I believe that all of us possess many gifts and abilities. The difficulty for me has been how to navigate being human and being in this dense three-dimensional environment. I don't know about you, but when I meditate or have a spiritual experience where I am connected to everything that is, I often have a difficult time wanting to and actually coming back. It is hard for me to not feel as free as I am when I am meditating and multi dimensionally traveling. When I remember that I am not able to shift things or move things as fast or in ways I know it is possible to do, I get frustrated.

It has taken me into my 50s to finally feel home in my body and on earth. I have learned that being on earth is about choice. It is about commitment to yourself and your journey. Being on earth is about learning to be okay with who you are, your own gifts, and being your own cheerleader. That last one has been particularly hard for me.

All of these things are important lessons. I used to spend so much time seeking validation about who I was and what my gifts and abilities were. I lost my way, as do many others. I got caught up in my ego for awhile. The truth is, it doesn't really matter what I can do. The only thing that really matters is that I am okay with who I am and being authentically me out in the world. We all matter, we are all light beings; we are all made up from the cosmos and the stars. We are never alone. There are so many forces with us each and every day, whispering to us and hoping we are listening. I have learned that it is about shutting out the noise, going inward and listening to my own internal GPS system. Do you have the strength to do that? Please, have faith in yourself and believe you are enough. You shifting and believing this causes a ripple that can affect all. Just like when you throw a stone into the water, the ripples spread out and are felt by the entire body of water. As human beings each one of us becoming our light causes the same ripple effect. We are all connected. We are all one. A change in one affects change in all.

I am working on freeing myself of the shackles of expectations of the world and of myself. This is the time on planet earth for all of us to be the most authentic versions of ourselves we can be. There is no looking back for humanity. As a consciousness, we have chosen and need to move forward. Humanity as a whole also needs every human being to wake up and break the shackles of control and complacency.

You will find that this is going to be a theme. I believe that we are all here to help our souls grow, and learn what we need to continue our soul's journey of evolution. I don't believe there are wrong choices. I believe different choices give us different opportunities to learn and grow. We have free will as human beings it is our right to make things as easy or difficult as we need them to be. We all have many paths that we can take. We get to choose which way we learn the lesson that we have outlined for our soul in this lifetime.

Welcome to the new you. The one you have been waiting for. My new motto is the three B's: Be, Breathe and Believe. Anything and everything is possible. Let go, trust and don't let limiting beliefs or fear stand in your way. There is no better time than now to start. Are you ready to take the journey into the unknown and rediscover your authentic self? I am. Let's get started.

Section Two
The Science Fiction Moments of My Life

I have been very fortunate in this lifetime, I can see, hear, see, feel and sometimes even smell. I can remember many of my past lives and am currently working with the multi dimensional beings to help earth evolve. So much to pull from and to share that I am unsure where to start.

Life has a way of happening; I am being guided at this time to continue the conversation and my story from book one.

It is interesting even though I know what I know, there are times where I think I am crazy and that what I am saying is way out there and then I realize it is not and has touched someone else. I was doing a radio interview with my publisher Ibbilane Press and we ended up talking about abortions and short lived lives. It is not something that I ever thought I would talk about on a radio interview and yet, there it was. I was talking about it. It has been my experience that when I am doing radio interviews I often times just end up channeling whatever information is needed and try not to judge what came out in the end. The information about abortion and short lived lives is that there are souls that want to have very different experiences some long and some short, and everything that happens we have agreed too before we come back and incarnate on earth. Earth is school this is where are souls are learning lessons, where we are remembering what we already know and then how to navigate having free will.

Experiences with Dolphins

One of the experiences I remember in the beginning of my re-opening was my room filling with water and then 3 dolphins came in. This was such a magical experience as I could easily communicate with them and understand what they were communicating to me. They were pinging me and playing with me and I felt at home. I have since had many experiences with telepathically communicating with dolphins. I have been fortunate as I can communicate with the dolphins from other dimensions as well. I especially like playing and communicating with the pink and gold dolphins from the 5th dimension. There is so much knowledge and wisdom that so many different beings in different dimensions hold.

I hate to break it to some of you out there but we are not alone in this universe and not even alone on earth. There are so many beings from so many dimensions helping us to evolve. I think of the dolphins. They are the Pleiadians, some say Sirians who are here with us to help us move forward as a consciousness. Think about it?

Swimming in the ocean is a lot like being in space. I think of the whales as the Acturians who also have much knowledge and healing abilities to share with us.

Abduction

There is so much that has been written on this subject. I was always skeptical about it until I started to have memories and also remembered dreams that I used to have. When I was younger I had dreams all the time of floating out of the window of my house. When I was younger and in therapy I remember drawing pictures and they were not of human beings. My therapists at the time never said a thing.

What I am about to write and talk about is completely open to your own interpretation. These are my memories, my stories, or what my soul needed to believe to move forward.

Over the years as I have done energy work, I started to have memories. I have always felt that I had a near death experience and my parents would always say nothing happened. Well here is what actually happened: One of the times that I was abducted I was close to being killed because I would not give up my light to the race that was trying to take it. My guides and angels on the other side took me out of my body because what the beings were doing was painful and almost killed me several times. All parties involved decided that I needed to go back. I was brought back to my body so that I could return to earth.

Again remember the title of part one of this series was almost "My Life as a Bad Science Fiction Movie."

I am not going to go into too many of the details, as when I start to talk about it or write about it, I feel physical pain in my body. I do not wish to do that anymore. Suffice it to say I have come to terms with all of it in a way that makes sense for me.   Other people who have had similar experiences may see it differently. I have never been one who needs people to believe what I believe. The only thing I ask is for everyone to keep an open mind and see what resonates as true for you.

One of the nightmares I used to have was being on a ship in a lab where they took my DNA. I was forced to watch them create these beings from my DNA hoping they would all have the gifts that I had and be able to do what I could do. The other memories were on ship with other humans and rows and rows of babies that were created from mixed DNA. Maybe this happened maybe it didn't. Maybe it was just a foreshadowing of information that our DNA is mixed with multi dimensional DNA. I find as a therapist that the truth is always somewhere in the middle.

In recent years more memories started to come back of them drilling into my skull to try and get the information that I have about the earth and the records of the earth. It was to no avail, as I was not going to give up that information. In this lifetime I have chosen service and the light and nothing and no one was going to pull me away from that.

Everything that we have done in all of our lifetimes was done so our souls could continue to develop and move forward. Again, maybe there were no aliens. Maybe it is my unconscious way of helping me see that I picked the light in this lifetime.

Whether it is being abducted, childhood trauma, abuse, whatever the situation, we have all created stories that make sense to our rational mind. Our stories make it so that we can deal with the experiences. Even though I know what I know, I am no different.

I know this was a lot for people to take in. I believe that it is time to just put everything on the table and then for each human being to make the choice about what they believe for themselves. Maybe they will understand what some similar experiences of theirs may have been.

Pain is pain and as humanity we are carrying around a great deal of it. It is time for many of us to learn to let go of the pain and the stories we have created and to learn to live in love and from the heart and the gut, and not our ego minds.

Thanks for keeping an open mind.

The Priestesses of Isis.

This is not something I thought I would ever put down in words as some people are going to consider this blasphemy. When Jesus was taken down from the Cross, he was not dead. Just like in the movie the princess bride, he was nearly dead. He was taken to the cave where the Priestesses of Isis helped heal his physical body and where he walked out 3 days later. He did arise in a way, showing us how powerful we are, especially when we are open to working together for a greater goal. The goal in this case being that humanity needed something to believe in, to help us move forward in our collective consciousness.

We are not the first incarnation of human beings; however we are the incarnation of human beings that is not going to blow itself up this time. There is a reason that the Middle East is a hotbed of activity and where many wars start. This is where the end of humanity has always taken place. This area on the globe needs massive amounts of healing energy so that we are able to transcend this as a human race.

The Priestesses of Isis or, as I sometimes like to call them, the women in white robes, were very influential and accomplished some major healings. Whenever the priestesses of Isis pop in I see them as group of 13 women standing in a circle in white robes.

We have been fed so many non-truths that we as a humanity no longer know what to believe in. Sometimes you need to unplug and just go within to see, feel, hear, or know what is there.
Learning to re-trust your own internal hunches. We have been conditioned to no longer trust ourselves and we are very disconnected from the rhythms of the earth and ourselves. This is why there are so many addictions and problems. We are loosing the ability to communicate as we develop more and more technology.

Healing

Over the years I have had seen and worked in many ancient healing temples. I understand how the ancient temples and ancient healings were done in many different civilizations. What I don't always understand, is what I am meant to do with all of the information I have been given. I understand why we have genetic disorders and what needs to be developed to cure them, I understand DNA at a level that I don't even know how to explain.

We are moving towards sound, frequency and vibrational healing, which is not going to make big Pharma happy as that is a billion dollar business. We all have the ability to heal ourselves. It is in our DNA. We do not trust ourselves enough to listen or we allow ourselves to believe that the non-mainstream techniques are crazy or woo woo. There are centuries of healers, known as shamans who understand the relationship with plant medicine, sound (drums, chanting) and a community coming together for vibration and frequency. If Big Pharma was really about healing wouldn't we see less illness and more people getting better? I understand that these are tough questions to answer, and maybe we need to start to have these conversations as a consciousness.

In Atlantis the end of the civilization was due to technology, greed misusing resources and power. We are headed that way as well. We need to find our heart again and the let our heart lead us as a consciousness. Re-learning to not be so controlled by the masses or afraid to stand our ground and follow our own believes. Consider the whole story of Mauna (yes the movie) about finding the heart that was stolen and returning it in order to thrive.

There is so much at stake right now. Most people do not understand what we are really trying to get too and how much they are being affected by things in our world. If what we are seeing in movies and TV is really 30-40 years behind what is actually happening in our world then we all have reason to be concerned. Take the movie The Matrix. It is all about control and making choices. Take the movie Allegiance about being being segregated as an experiment to see what would happen. So many signs if we are willing to see them.

Think about the meaning of stop lights in our culture. A red light means stop. The chakra color Red is about survival, tribal beliefs and going along with the masses. This is our root chakra. The yellow light means caution. The yellow or solar plexus chakra is being in your power is a caution. Interesting, when you start to see everything as signs and what it means to you and our society. The Green light means go. The heart chakra guides you to follow and listen to your heart and go from that space.

I am not sure where we are going as a humanity, I just know we are capable of so much more than what we are currently doing. We sometimes need to unplug, be present with ourselves and be present with others.

Healing Classes

Knowing what I know, even though I was not always consciously aware created a lot of interesting dynamics for me when I would take classes. The teachers would ask me why I was there, you already know these things and my presence in the class would make them really uncomfortable. Here are some of the examples:

Reiki was the first healing class I took as it is for many people. When I got to level 2 and was being initiated I started to see multi dimensional beings in the room with me. It was my first experience with physically seeing them since I was younger. At first, I was a little frightened and quickly realized these beings were here to help me not hurt me. I know that is way out there for some of the people reading this and for others they will be comforted by this. I think it is important to speak your truth whatever that may be. I did not dare talk to my teacher about this at the time for fear of what she would say or do. My experience in the class appeared to be so different from everyone else.

When I took DNA theta healing I had a different experience. I had done so much work in the class, my third eye was wide open and I was not doing well. The teacher of the class looked at me and said well you know how to fix that, and I need to help with these other people. No, I did not know on a conscious level how to fix it. I left and walked around for a couple of days with my third eye blown wide open and getting many messages not knowing what to do with them. I had an appointment with a woman I was working with in the Akashic records later in the week and my third eye was soothed and parts of it rebuilt. Needless to say, I never took another class with that teacher.

When I took quantum touch I had the technique figured out in 10 minutes and had to sit through an entire day of the class. The teacher of that class again kept asking why I was there when I obviously already understood it. I don't remember how I answered at the time, and was frustrated for being called out. I needed to learn how to bring the energy from this technique through my physical body in this lifetime. Knowing and understanding it at a higher vibration and frequency was not enough, sometimes it needs to come through in 3rd dimensional ways.

I took an angelic healing class. The teacher was offering some private sessions for an extra fee. I decided to have one. As the teacher was working on me energetically, Ashtar of the Galactic Federation of the light came in through my crown chakra and was in my body with me. It was a very strange experience and feeling to say the least. I told Ashtar that there was not enough room in my physical body so he was going to have to leave. I told him he could stay close by. When the teacher was done I asked if he saw what had happened he said yes, and did not say anything further. Another experience different from everyone else and no one to talk to and process it with.

I do not believe that anything any of these teachers did was malicious in any way. At the same time, all of this left a very lasting effect on me. I did not want to take any more classes nor did I want to teach. I have taken several classes since these experiences and I have learned to just sit quietly in classes and not say anything unless I am asked a direct question. As I became more comfortable with my gifts, I have learned to balance being silent and sharing in classes.

In one of my healing classes there was a group of us that had become friends. One of them was diagnosed with a brain tumor. The other four of us opened the Akashic Records to see if there was anything we could do to help. We all sat quietly for a long time, I did not want to be the one to do the healing this time. I wanted it desperately to be one of the others. I kept sitting there, silently saying "not me", feeling this queasy feeling in my stomach,   The next thing I know, I hear "may I approach your head?" come out of my mouth.   I approached my friend. I put my hand in the front and back of her head where the tumor was. I could see the tumor. I knew exactly where it was and what needed to happen. The next thing I know, I feel like I am shooting ice out of my hands and my body temperature dropped. I became the vessel to freeze and shrink the tumor. After the procedure or healing was completed it took many hours to get my body temperature back up to normal.

I used to be involved in Healing Sundays using the model they use in the Casa in Brazil which I referenced in my first book. There were so many times that I had experiences while doing healings. In this instance I remember seeing white light actually shoot out my hands into the other person's body almost like lightening bolts. I would see whoever it was on a table, and wherever there was a problem or an issue would light up like in an x-ray or CT scan. Then I would be directed on what to do or where to position my hands. I was being guided by the same Doctors that work in the casa in Brazil.

In some of my sessions with my Akashic record teacher, I would need to ground her and work with her while she was working with me. I would see elementals holding her feet down. My teacher would say the energy was too high she couldn't manage. One of the times I was there, I literally saw rainbow energy shooting out of my hands. Sometimes it is hard when you keep surpassing your teachers and they have a hard time letting go.

This was a common theme for me though, helping the teachers who were trying to help me. Intuitively I just knew and saw things that they did not. They were always asking me questions, as my vibration and frequency was often too much for them to handle so I needed to moderate it for them so as not to blow them out of the water.
This always left me questioning who am I, why am I here and terrified to be a healer and to actually touch someone for fear of what I could do.

It has taken many years and I am finally starting to do some hands on healing work again. I have let go of the fear and am open to be the conduit I am meant to be. There are so many different ways to be a healer and to use gifts. I am learning what mine are.

We all have our own journey and we need to find the strength in ourselves to have the courage to take that journey. It took me many years to be able to be comfortable and confident in myself.

The last example I want to share was in another class. I went into oneness with one of my classmates and we were just in pure joy and laughing and the teacher was annoyed because it was disrupting the flow of the class. When we started to come back to the third dimension someone in the class said something that started us laughing again brining us back to that heightened stated of bliss. The teacher eventually gave up and just let it go, because now the whole class was vibrating higher.

Part of my goal for writing this down is to help others have a voice and find people they can start to have these conversations with. It is very important to have a support system around you.

Bilocating

I have always been able to bilocate. Not something I have chosen to share with a lot of people until now. It started when I was really young. I can remember being in two places at the same time.

When I was younger I had a white pedal car. I thought that this car was what allowed me to bilocate as it happened a lot when I was in that car. Later and as I got older I realized it was not the car that allowed me to bilocate it was being out in nature, being in motion and connecting to everything. This is what causes me to just leave and travel.

When I was at camp at the age of 11 or 12, I was standing on the porch of the main building. The next thing I knew I was talking and playing with friends on the side of my house until someone called my name at camp and I was yanked back into my body. I will never forget that feeling of being yanked back into my body it was so forceful.

One of my teachers used to go to Brazil to work with John of God a couple of times a year. I would go into a deep meditation and I remember walking around the casa. When my teacher came back she asked me why I didn't tell her I was going to Brazil she would have helped me make the arrangements. This was the first time that I realized that other people could see me when I was bilocating. I could describe the casa and what the casa was built on and even the stars, or shall we say light ships, that were in the sky. I have never physically been there but I feel as if I have.

One of my friends was taking a healing class. She wanted me to go to class with her, so I went into a meditation and was in class with her. Again, not really aware that other people could see me when I do this, and her teacher asked me to leave the class.

As I continue to get older and more comfortable with my gifts I can coexist in both places rather peacefully and am no longer yanked back to my body when someone calls my name. This is nice because I did not like that feeling of being yanked back in. It was very jolting.

I am sure others of you who are reading this can relate to some of this. I have learned that often times I am the one to get conversations going. It is something I have finally become more comfortable with and do not drag my feet as much as I used too.

Ice Beings

This is when it is helpful to remember some of your past lives, so that when you get channeled information it doesn't seem so over the top. This would be one of those messages.

I made a pact in Atlantis with the Ice Beings to keep all the Atlantean secrets until it was time for humanity to be able to receive them again. There are others who also hold this information and frequency.
There was a ceremony that took place transferring the knowledge. There was a holographic mandala created with the specific frequency and vibration to keep this information safe. All of this took place before Atlantis jumped dimensions and ceased to exist in the 3rd dimension.
The holographic mandala has much information besides the Atlantean records stored in it and as we a consciousness get to where we need to be this information will be decoded by those who hold the key.
The ice beings have shown and given me many different healing techniques which I feel

privileged to have experienced and fortunate to be able to use with others to promote well being. Sometimes as humans it is like opening Pandora's Box. We are not ready for the technology as our hearts are not in the right place. If humanity would have access to this right now many would try and misuse the power. As human beings become more heart centered and live from their heart space and realize that all is truly connected and all is one, we may reach a point where we are ready for this again. One of the messages I have been receiving over and over again is that it is my time to teach. Now, if I could only figure out what it is I am supposed to be teaching and helping humanity with that would be amazing. It has been my experience that holding so much knowledge and secrets of the universe it makes it difficult to narrow it down at times.

One of the things that I learned from working with the ice beings is that some of the energy portals or mandalas that come through are information to help humanity shift. Coded pieces in time depending on what the person needs when looking at the image. It is always interesting when I sit down to write as I often discover more pieces to the puzzle of what my multi dimensional art is really about.

Control Panels and Science Fiction Moments

Many years ago I was instructed to get an iPad. I didn't know why when I first got it what it was going to unlock. Again, remember the working title of this series was my life as a science fiction movie. This part really delves into that. I needed the iPad in order to learn how to use my multi dimensional control panel. I would describe the control panel as a semi circle with many screens and knobs. You could say that it looks like a star trek control panel. I used to be fortunate to see this panel all the time, now I think it is just part of my consciousness. I am not always aware anymore when I am looking at it or changing and shifting things. From this panel I can control all the crystals of the earth and repair damage to ones. For example, the Bermuda triangle. This was an Atlantean crystal that was misfiring and transporting people to different dimensions. It has now been repaired and restored to its proper level of functioning, frequency, and vibration.

Some of the information I am going to write about in this section is going to be difficult for a lot of people to swallow.

Let's take the Andes mountains and plane crashes. One night I was going to bed and was really tired. There was a little Peruvian boy who came to me and said that I needed to go with him he needed my help. I said I was really tired could it wait. A couple days later I was in my Akashic Records working with my instructor and had Déjà vu. This Peruvian boy was there again. I had forgotten about it as I was exhausted. He asked if I would go with him now. I said yes. We went to the crystals in the Andes mountains some were not where they were supposed to be and causing interference with planes. They caused a dimensional perspective issues where planes where not judging depth and perception appropriately causing the plane crashes. We have not heard of any plane crashes since then and that was five years ago or more.

I am also fortunate to know about the crystals in Antarctica and how different forces keep moving them and it is my job to go back and rebalance them. I am a record keeper of the earth. I have been here many times before and it is my job to protect the earth, the grids and the crystals from forces that do not want to use them for good. I am putting myself at risk writing all of this but it is time, don't you think, for us all to take our power back.

My control panel allows me to communicate with many dimensional beings and things happening in the universe. Just to be clear, this is a multi dimensional control panel and does not exist in this third dimensional world, in case anyone reading this wants to try and access it or take it. Only certain frequencies, vibrations, and human beings can access it.

When I had my re-opening which I detailed in the first book, I used to see the pyramids in Egypt a lot and what they are really for. However, as a humanity we are still not ready for the secrets they hold.

I have been in the secret rooms in the sphinx I know where the records of Atlantis are. Sometimes holding all of this information can seem overwhelming as how do you know what to share and with whom to share it.

Since I am writing about this I am going to write about all of it. Depending on what you believe or have been told, there are agencies that watch over people like me and there are black helicopters that you cannot see that are watching. I remember one morning getting up early for work. My brother was up and said what is with the helicopter hovering over our house. I wasn't sure anyone else could see or hear them.

I have also been given information on how we can cure genetic disorders and how if we continue to screw up and manipulate our electro magnetic field we are going to do serious damage to our civilization just like in Atlantis.

These places and times are real... they are just in a different dimension now on the earth but they existed and impacted the earth and our consciousness...

It is time for us all to awaken to the dream within the dream. I think of our reality like a star trek holodeck. We are creating all of this. It is time we create something different. There are still some control tactics used on us but more and more of us are awakening and it is time to help others. There really is no such thing as fear. We created that as well. It is time to move out of the duality of good versus evil or light and dark and live in the multi dimensional healing matrix that is available to all of us.

Another example is the Akashic Records of the earth. I have had to move the Akashic records of the earth many times, as forces of let's just say not the light, try and get them and use them to their advantage. The same with the ancient scrolls that are being found in and around Africa. If you have a high enough frequency and vibration, they are in plain sight and can be read. All I can say is I am fortunate enough to have access to all this information. My question or dilemma is always how to use this information in the most responsible was as possible and holding for the highest good and vibration of all.

The wish for this section is to take what you believe and what resonates for you and to let go of the rest. I have always been reluctant to fully put all of this information out there. I have come to learn that I need to be authentically me, if I expect or teach others in how to be authentic. Being authentic means being true to who you are and trusting that you will be okay and be taken care of.

One of the other things I want to share in this section is that my images do represent and hold many of the same frequencies as crop circles. You may say that the same multi dimensional beings are working with me that create crop circles. Again crop circles are a wake up call for us to unlock consciousness to help humanity move forwards.

When I was taking all the opening to intuition courses I would drive back and forth to Green Lake, Wisconsin. I always had a vision of a learning center/hub. I always believed it would be created here on earth in the third dimension and have realized that it already exists in another dimension and I travel to it all the time. Later I came to realize that this learning center is tied to Lemuria and Atlantis.

The last thing I want to talk about in this section is the galactic meetings of the Federation of Light that happen in the Sphinx every week. There are reasons why Egypt does not let parts of some of the ancient wonders to be open to the public. There is also a multi dimensional transporter in the sphinx were beings come in and out.

Being a Medium

Being a Medium has its plusses and minuses. What I am going to share here really happened. I have not changed any of the details. Ever since I was little I have always known when people and pets were going to cross over. For people in my family I would have a dream about a funeral. I would not always remember the dream until I was at the funeral and having déjà vu. The other thing that has started to happen as I have gotten older is that my relatives who have crossed over have started to visit me and communicate with me before it is time.

I have lost both of my parents within two years and I'm now trying to find my way in the world without their physical presence. It is true what they say that when you lose both of your parents, regardless of the type of relationship it was, you feel like an orphan. Well, that is how I feel right now. I never thought that would be true with what I know but it is.

I am going to share my journey with each of my parents as they were both poignant and so much to take in. I was just starting to move past the grief of my mother dying then my father died. I knew it was coming for about 3 months and no one else believed me. The lesson I have learned or should say I am finally learning is to trust myself because in the end I was correct not the medical professionals.

With my maternal grandfather a few weeks before he died, his sister who had transitioned earlier, came every night at the same time they would talk. The day my maternal grandfather died I had four really bad bloody noses and knew that day he was going to die. He had experienced some complications and the hospital that caused them was sending him to a nursing home. My grandfather always said the day you put me in a nursing home will be the day I die. He died later that day right after he got to the nursing home.

With my maternal grandmother, I had conversations with my grandfather and with her about seeing my grandfather. These conversations made her really uncomfortable because she knew it was getting close to the end. My maternal grandmother was a very strong, amazing woman and Hospice said they had never seen someone in complete control of her facilities even though her body was shutting down. I had a very strong bond with my grandmother. There were nights where I would hear her calling to me and wake up with her telling me it was time to let go. I told my family they needed to say goodbye and give her permission to go as she was holding on for all of us. These conversations never went well in my family and I was usually told I did not know what I was talking about it. My grandmother had a strong bond with one of her doctors who was out of town and had promised to come see her when he got back. There was no way that she was going to make it another week. I told the Hospice nurse what she was waiting for. The nurse leaned over and said to my grandmother, your doctor called and you know he would want you to be at peace. An hour and a half later she transitioned.

My paternal grandmother had Alzheimer's and was often in an agitated state during the last few years. As I became more comfortable with my abilities I would meditate and journey to her to the light to show her there was no fear and she was eventually able to let go.

Again sometimes these blessings are a curse and sometimes a gift. It is a curse or difficult is when it is your family and you know and everyone else tells you that you are wrong it is not happening. It has been a blessing as I have been able to help so many of my friends losing a loved one with dignity, grace and timing.

The more difficult and still really hard situations for me to have helped in were with my parents. As some of you who have read volume 1 know I did not have the best most supportive parents especially when it came down to me talking about what I know and believe. I have lost both parents now and as I write this I am very much in the grieving process and so much has been triggered.

I helped many friends transition as well. One of my friends when I went to see her towards the end, opened her eyes and said I have been waiting for you master. Have to admit that freaked me out a little. I went into meditative states over the next couple of days and took her to the light so she could see what it was like. Her husband and son asked me when I thought she would transition and I told them. It turned out that the information I gave them was true.

Then I lost two close friends and my mother all within 9 months. I have to admit that was a very difficult time for me. Especially with everything I felt at the time.

One of my closet friends who I helped keep here for awhile per her request was getting close to transition. I went to see her in the hospital and I could not stay. It was so close I could feel it and I became very activated. When she transitioned, I got the phone call at 5am as they could not reach her son. He had his phone off. I didn't even know that I was on the list. Sometimes we have a bigger impact on people's lives than we think we do.

I lost another friend to cancer shortly after that. I considered him to be a father figure and a mentor. This was a hard loss for me. He had called me before he went back into the hospital to transition and told me he was not leaving. I was on a road trip a few days later and I knew he transitioned. I could feel it and his spirit and I knew he was free. A couple minutes later I got a phone call from a mutual friend telling me he transitioned. I already knew. This friend who was an amazing healer and helped people all over the world came and helped me with my mother from the other side her last few nights. I felt so grateful and so blessed. Later I found out from other people how much he had trusted me and relied on me and let me work with him energetically. This was another opportunity for me to learn the lesson that I know some things and to trust myself. Here was this amazing healer with clients all over the world coming to me for help.

I will start with the passing of my mother since chronologically that came first. My mother always had a fear of death since as a little girl she became very sick and almost died. She also was not fond of doctors from that experience. My mother was afraid to be buried in the group and had bought crypts because of that fear. When my grandmother died my mother's views of death started to change. Since she was so close with her mother, now she wanted to be buried near her.

The journey with my mother was a difficult one for me based on my beliefs versus what she believed. As her cancer progressed and knew it was getting close to time for her to be leaving which I was not and still am not prepared for. I started to have conversations with her about death and dying because I know she needed to have them. Towards the end she was in ICU and there were discussions of a DNR and power of attorney. My mother signed the DNR because she did not want any tubes and at the same time was very scared and I could feel all of it. My mother made me the power of attorney because ultimately she knew that I would make the hard choices and decisions. I had the dream of a funeral and knew the time was getting closer. I started talking to her about if any of her relatives were in communication with her. As hard as it was for me and her to have the conversation we did. She said one of her great aunts had been visiting her.

My mother did not want to die in a Hospital and wanted to come home. Arrangements were made and hospice was involved. My mother came home on August 10th. I am including a lot of dates as I write this because they will become important when I talk about my father's transition.

We, her family, did not know we needed around the clock care we were ill prepared for her to come home. There were many hospice staff and home health care staff who were involved. All I kept saying is that if we do not figure it out she will be back in the hospital in 3 days. Again, important to pay attention to that number as well. She came home on a Thursday. I had made the appointment with a funeral home for

Friday morning just to get some details, as there was no insurance. My father had cancelled all the policies and we were going to have to come up with the money from thin air.

I made the arrangements on August 12, 2016 picked out everything got a total and had started a go fund me page to help with the hospice and nursing care costs we were starting to rack up. My mother had multiple myeloma and I believe the cancer was everywhere at this point. Friday morning she got up and went to the bathroom and we had to call paramedics to help her get back in bed. She never got up again and really was not conscious much after that. I believe her other collar bone was fractured from that incident.

We did not have anyone at night so I stayed up every night with her and could feel people from the other side working with her trying to ease the pain and suffering she was in. I was giving her all the medications and was calling hospice every couple of hours as she was in so much pain. By Saturday night one of the hospice nurses came and she was transferred to the Hospital early Sunday Morning August 14th. The doctors came in and told us it was imminent, which I already knew. We called family and friends and all who wanted to say goodbye. Everyone went home around dinnertime and I went back. I shut off the elevator music they had playing as she hated it. I just sat next to her bed telling her it was okay to go and go towards the light. I saw my great aunt reach down for her and clearly heard my mother say no, not while my daughter is here . I heard 9:03 pm. One of my friends came and sat with me and it was 8:50pm. I told her that we had to leave. My mother was going to transition at 9:03. As hard as it was for me I left. I wanted so badly to run back upstairs to her room at the hospital at 9pm but I honored her and I went home and got ready for bed. At 9:45pm the phone rang from the hospital to tell me my mother transitioned.

I was really struggling feeling like I had helped kill her by giving her all the medication which a lot of care givers experience. I took advantage of the free grief counseling hospice offered. My appointment was at 9am and the therapist came out to get me a few minutes early. I started to tell him the story and that the death certificate says 9;15am but she transitioned at 9:03. When I was done telling my experience and what happened he looked up at the clock and it was 9:03am. Just a sign of confirmation.

My mother transitioned on August 14th and her funeral was on August 17, 2016 at 10am. Again that is going to be significant.

I am still struggling with the loss of my mother and now I am having to be there for my father which was another conflicted relationship. My father did not do well with my mother's transition and did not pay anything or do anything to make the funeral arrangements. It all fell to me. My father also became difficult and I never got to grieve because he kept stating he was having a heart attack and refused to go to Shiva and lots of other things I do not need to get into.

After my mother transitioned, I sat down and was doing some writing. One of the things I talked about in book one was my mother having a stillborn when I was 4 or 5 years old. This message came through from that being who would have been my younger brother.

Dearest Sister,

I know we never met on the physical plane of existence. I want you to know that I have been with you your whole life. We are very connected. While I was in our mother's womb are spirits talked all the time. You knew that I would never be born into physical form. You supported and loved me and now I support and love you.

Please know that when our mother's spirit reconnected with mine there was an immense healing. You helped her on your side and I helped her on this side. Just know you are seen, you are loved and that you light the way for so many. Please do not dim your light anymore.

It is time to be fully you just like when you were a little girl.

Our mother and grandparents all support you and love you. Please take it all in because you have such a huge capacity to love, let us give back to you and fill you from the other side.

Your loving younger brother.

Fast forward 2 years. My father is admitted to the Hospital on Saturday August 4th.

I knew it was getting close the end as I started to see and have conversations with my Grandmother rose. That was a very conflicted relationship for me when she was alive, and watching her be by his side and try and comfort him in the last couple of weeks is an image I will never forget. Our bonds do not go away just because we have left the physical plane. We are still all connected. I know my father will continue to look out for me from the other side and that I will continue to have conversations with him.

There were also so many synchronicities that I looked at as signs that his life was coming to an end. The first was as most of you know my mother transitioned on August 14th two years ago. When he was taken to Lutheran General there are 30 rooms in the ER. When I got to the desk I was told he was in room 14. I knew something was up.

The first day he was in the hospital we got several phone calls from him to take him out of there, they were trying to hurt him and he just wanted to go home. The last call that day I let go to voice mail. It had been an emotional roller coaster of the day and I needed to get some sleep. I am so grateful I let it go to voice mail as it was my father calling saying goodbye and wishing me well. It brings me to tears every time I listen to it. Here is the message. I still can't listen to it without crying. Keep in mind when reading this my father was in restraints and medicated due to his agitation. When spirit wants us to get something there is always a way.

"Hi Gail, this is your dad. I am glad I got a chance to call you. I love you very much. I have always loved you very much. I will miss you terribly. I hope I was a good dad even though I know I wasn't. I love you so much sweetheart. I don't know if I will get your brother, please, please tell him I love him very much. Take care and have a great life. Enjoy yourself some. Don't work yourself to death. Just enjoy yourself. Let some things go. Take good care. I am sorry I could not have done more for you. I love you both so much. Take good care sweetheart. Enjoy your life. Please enjoy your life and have a good life. Don't work so hard and just have a good life. I will think about you always. I love you and I love your brother. Thank you so much. Have a good one."

Sunday I went to the Hospital and I asked to sign DNR paperwork as he was delirious and was not coherent, he was physically restrained as he kept trying to pull his tubes out and was really agitated. The staff helped me fill out the paperwork. There was something really important in doing it and not waiting I just did not know what it was yet.

I went to work on Monday and left a little early to go to the hospital. I had just walked up onto the unit and heard a code blue. I instantly knew it was my father. I was standing outside his room while it was happening in tears. He started to breathe again and seemed to come out of it. My brother and I decided to take him off the heart monitors and worked with the staff. He was in and out of it. I still believed it was going to be a fast transition and no one else around me did.

On Friday Hospice was called in and my brother and I met with them to sign the paperwork. They hospice Nurse who was older and I pointed to my brother. She asked my brother if he would sign the paperwork and he said no let her, meaning me, do it. Again I was made power of attorney to make all the difficult decisions.

Friday on my way home from work I needed some food so I stopped at the store. The total was 50.19 and as many of you know the number for my parents for 50years was 677-5019... Signs that he wanted to go home.

I made arrangements to meet with the same funeral director to start to talk about options. The meeting turned out to be the same day 2 years earlier I met with him to discuss my mothers death. August 12th. I made all of the arrangements and told him that I did not think it would be long.

Monday Morning August 13th the night nurse called and said he was not doing well, it would be a good idea to come on and see him. I got there and the day nurse told me he was doing better. I spoke with hospice and they said the signs aren't there yet and I told the hospice nurse why I was pretty sure it was going to be really soon.

Tuesday August 14th. Again got a call and went to the hospital before work, this time the hospice nurse was there and she said he had turned and did not think it was going to be long. They were going to move him up to the hospice floor in the hospital. I said my goodbyes and then went to work to make the arrangements to be out for the next of the week. There was some part of me that was just so sure even though my family was in denial.

Tuesday night I had a session with someone I was working with. I went into a deep meditation and kept seeing my father half in and half out of his body. In the meditation, I took my father's had and we went towards the light, I had done this before with many other people which is why I have referred to myself as the angel of death before. We went towards the light. I actually saw parts of his life reviews and just kept reassuring him it would be okay. I took my father's hand and put it in my mother's hand. Now, I need to share that towards the end of their lives they did not like each other much and my father had done a lot of things to be worried about what he was going to have to face when he transitioned. I came out of my mediation and it was profound. I went back to the hospital after that and my brother was there too and we have not always had the best relationship either. We had a very civil conversation and out father got to see that we would both be okay.

I left knowing that I would not see my father alive again in physical form. I had the oddest vision the whole day. When I energetically looked in on my father he was half in and half out of his body. That was new for me to see. I did not sleep at all that night as I kept waiting for the phone call. At some point in the early hours of the morning my room just lit up with light like the horizon a brilliant flash of light and so much peace. I know that is when my father transitioned.

Shortly after that around 5;30am the phone rang. It was the hospital telling me he had passed and asked me if I wanted to come. I told the hospice staff he needed to give me about 10 minutes. As much as I was prepared for this to happen when I got the call I just started sobbing. I called and told my brother. Hospice called back I said I did not want to go to the Hospital the funeral home could come and I would see him there.

My father died early morning on August 15h and I did not understand until the day of the funeral as to why it was not on the 14th. My paternal grandfather died on his son's birthday and his son died on his birthday which was August 15th.

Two more synchronicities. My father's funeral was on August 17, 2018 at 10am exactly two years after my mother's August 17, 2016 10am, and same funeral home.

The last synchronicity was that the death certificate was picked up on August 23rd, which was my mother's birthday. It was evident that family bonds transcend time and our logical brains.

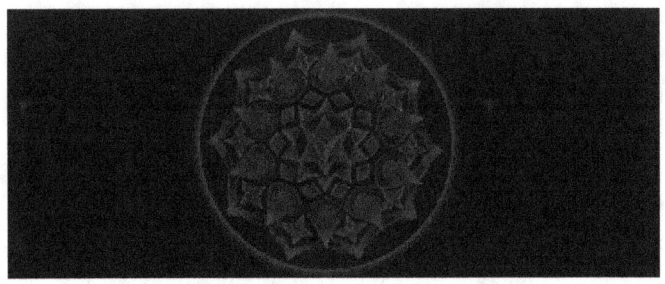

Mandalas

I am going to end this section of the book by talking about the images I create. In my first book, "I don't know How I know . . . I just know" I talked about how I started to create the mandalas. As a friend of mine pointed out, I have never talked about this topic further. I am going to share what creating these mandalas or portals means to me and how it is one of my favorite things to do.

When the process first started and I started drawing, I was flooded with information and seeing 100s of mandalas. Over the years the process has changed somewhat. I don't see the images before I create them anymore. Well, that is not entirely true. When something in the world happens and I am not in a space where I can create the mandala I will still see it floating in space until I can get it down on paper.

The energy of the mandalas or portals I create could be likened to crop circles. They have a very similar frequency and vibration. The information probably comes from the same place or from the same groups of multi dimensional beings.

Each Mandala or portal I create and bring forth has its own frequency, vibration, and messages. It is always amazing to me which ones resonate with who. Sometimes after I create one I will back away from my drawing table and be like, where did that come from that is so awesome. One of the things that I quickly learned about the images I create is that I have a great deal of help from my guides, spirit team, Angels, Arch Angels, Multi Dimensional Beings and source. I know that I am just the conduit who is fortunate to bring these energies to our planet at this time.

When things happen in the world, I create an image, and will often times put it on social media to reach as many people as I can as the energy needs to disperse amongst the planet.

I have hidden behind the mandalas for a long time and now it is time to take center stage, and be the most authentic version of myself I can be. This is why there are mandalas that are attached to each section and sub section in the book to hold the frequency and vibration of the words in that section. Mandalas or portals are getting through to our unconscious minds, often giving us clues, hints and information that our conscious mind is unable to pick up.

I am so blessed and fortunate to get to create these images and to teach others to tap into themselves to create them for themself or for gifts to people. I do not believe mine is the only way and I believe there is enough in the universe for all of us. If someone starts creating amazing images that does not take away from what mine do that only means there is now more energy on the planet, which can benefit all of us.

Everything in the universe and on Earth, and the earth itself has a vibration and frequency. I take that vibration and frequency and turn it into a portal or mandala that can then unlock the messages that we need. We cannot see frequency and vibration with the naked eye yet and I can and then create these images using the principles of sacred geometry, love and light. Once the image is created it does not matter how many times it is copied or what medium the image is in the energy, frequency and vibration is sealed in it. I wish I could explain how that happens. The truth of the matter is that I really don't want to know how it happens because I really enjoy the magic of it.

I am blessed and privileged to share this gift with the world.

When I first started creating them it was an endless stream that never stopped. I worked over 40 hours a week as a therapist was taking an intuition class driving several hours every day and yet every night I would create 3-4 big images. At the time I didn't understand what I was drawing and when I look back now, they were more medical pictures to help with different systems in the body and our energetic field. Again, sometimes things just come through me that I do not understand why I understand it but I do.

Everyone tells me I should draw them differently or make them free floating. My brain works very logically and rationally. I have a lazy eye and have been told that I really only use one of my physical eyes and that I have no depth perception. This is fascinating to me because if you look at my images they all have depth and are multi dimensional.

Again, we don't need to understand things sometimes. Sometimes the gift is in trusting the process to get us where we need to go. I have learned to do this. It is interesting what comes up when you start to do your work and move forwards. One of the things that came up for me was that the colored pencils that I wanted were very expensive and I did not feel worthy of spending that money on them. I have since gotten past that and have most brands of colored pencils that are made now. I remember having a conversation with my mother while she was alive about it. I just kept saying I can't do it, I can't spend that kind of money on colored pencils. I am glad that I have and continue to do so, because nothing in this world brings me more joy than creating these images and helping humanity shift and move forwards.

Section Three:
Channelings: Messages to Humanity

In this section going to include some prayers, thoughts, messages and channelings that came through to help humanity as well as each and every human being. We are all one and we are all unique. The overwhelming theme seems to be about love, connecting and being who we are meant to be.

Prayer:

May you be blessed with Divine Grace, Love and Light to fill your heart, spirit and soul for now and always.
May the power of the universe and creation carry you through every day.
May you learn to see the beauty and lessons in all that surrounds you.

Connection:

We are connected and all part of divine grace and love.
It is time to decide what the new world, global connectedness, and healing are going to look like.
Go forth and spread love, light, peace, grace and joy.
You have a voice – use it in peace and love, not fear and hate.
Speak your truth.
Stay pure of heart.
Be a champion for peace.
Light the way for others.

To the World:

We are one race, the human race.
We are all love.
Some of us have lost our way and are caught in the lower frequencies.
Some of us have been able to rise to the occasion to continue to shine light and love out in the world to wake others up.
There truly is no darkness, as we all possess the light in our hearts if we tune into the frequency and vibration.
We are all connected.
We all have a heart and it beats with a rhythm and force to sustain and nurture us so we can continue to live and breathe.
Our lungs are our wings they help us take flight and exist.
Our blood and nervous system are our life force or chi.
Our bones, muscles and flesh are our vehicle to navigate this dimension in.
We are energy. We are all part of the one. There is no separation.
Be, Believe and Breathe. This is what we need to focus on right now.
Miracles are possible.

Just believe and never lose hope.
As there is breath in your body there is hope.

Dear Ones:

Now is the time of great change. Keep faith and be the light that you are.
All will be tested. Learn to follow your internal guidance.
Dig deep to find peace amongst the chaos.
Now is the time to celebrate who you are and are becoming.
Be joyful. Share your full heart with others and let go of fear.
Fully embrace the lightness of your soul and spirit.
Each and every one of you matter and have value.
Even when you are lost, even when you struggle, you are never truly alone.
Believe in yourself you are an amazing work of art.
Treasure you.
You have the capacity to tune in and hear profound messages from your soul, spirit and source every day.
Trust what you are receiving. You have your own internal GPS system.
Please remember this during the next few months, all for one and one is all.

Dear Ones:

Today is a day of resetting and rebalancing.
Many of you who are sensitive to energies are always are of this.
There is so much going on in the world right now, seen and unseen.
Have faith that all is being worked out in divine order.
Have faith and trust your light and your path.
It is important to not lose your way during this time.
Breathe Deep.
Center Yourself.
Drink plenty of water.
Allow the shifts to happen.
The more you fight them the harder they will be.

Dear Ones:

Today we want to talk about hope.
(HOPE = HEARTS, OPEN, PERFECTLY, EVERY TIME)
Another important four letter word.
Hope is about being human and seeing all the possibilities that exist.
Continue to believe even when there is a part of you that does not.
The world right now is going through huge transformations, as is each and every human being.
Have hope. You are enough.
Have and keep hope that you matter.
Have hope that all is unfolding for you and the planet's highest good right now, even when you don't know what that is or what it is going to look like.

Dear Ones:

Taking the next steps about being centered, grounded and allowing yourself to be in flow.
Don't get bogged down with things you have no control over.
Let go of expectations and outcomes, as this is where suffering comes from.
Be in the moment, that is all you really have.
Learn to be present in your life.
Breathe in and out.
Focus on your breath filling your body, mind, soul and spirit with light.
Life is about balance, peace, harmony and joy.
Meditate or calm yourself every day.
Go inside, as this is where all the answers you are seeking lie.
Listen.

Dear Ones:

As you leave here take the love, light and grace you feel and spread it to others.
 We are all connected, we are one, we are part of divine grace – there is no separateness.
There is a collective whole.
It is time for others to wake up to the dream within the dream. Go forth and spread the light, love and grace.
Learn to touch others as you have been touched by this experience.
Now is the time as there needs to be global connectedness and healing.
Live and speak your truth.
You each have a voice, use it.
Stay true and pure of heart.
Light the way for others.
Be a champion of peace.

Dear Ones:

Trust all will be revealed.
Keep dreaming and allowing.
We are proud of you.
It is time to get through any doubts and worthiness issues.
You are all bright white lights that have lost their way at times.
Go within that is where your answers lie.
You have so much to offer.
Dive into yourself and let that light shine.
You are loved and cared for deeply.
Trust all is well, it is.
You are shedding the illusions.

Dear Ones:

It is time for humanity to raise its consciousness and find its heart again.

There is no better time than the holiday season when there is good will and gratitude. Just know that once this transition takes place, human consciousness will be in a whole new paradigm.

So many beautiful changes are ahead and sometimes you have to see the ugly before you can see the beauty.

Plus, the beauty is in the eye of the beholder. Humanity has some challenges ahead and now you need to choose to deal with and face these challenges. As humanity does this more light will come to the earth and to human beings.

Each human being has a divine spark and purpose.

It is time for human consciousness to remember you are all connected to everything that is there is no separateness.

Go out and encourage each other to be the lights that you all are.

Dear Ones:

As the changes on the earth take place, it is important for each of you to take care of your physical body.
It is time to start to listen to internal guidance and disconnect from technology.
Technology is causing a shift in consciousness and not necessarily one for the better. Take time every day to breathe and just quiet your mind and slow down your breathing.
Take time to center yourself.
Take time to remember what you are grateful for.
Pay attention to the people and the messages around you, there are signs everywhere.
Laugh even when you do not feel with it.
Find others on a similar path and connect.
Finding your tribe and your place in this world helps your autonomic nervous system stay in balance.
Realize you are learning and playing your part every day for the greater good.
Find what brings you joy and do more of that.
Let your light shine brightly.
Be who you are.

To Humanity:

We need you to have courage and faith that you can get through these times.
You must not give up.
You must persevere.
This is the time you need to show up.
Be the light you are and are meant to be.
Let it shine brightly to help others who may have lost their way.
It takes all of you to make the shift.
You each have your own role to play.
Now is the time to play it.
Breathe and jump in.

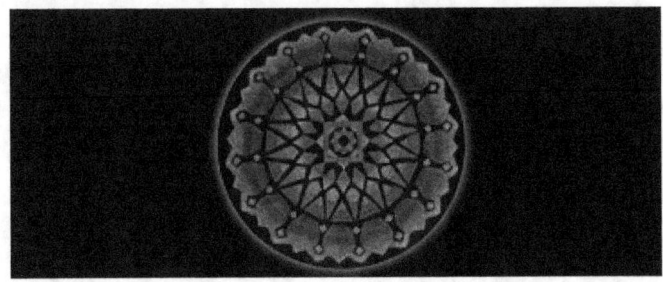

To Humanity:

The universe is presenting itself in new ways.
As more and more awaken more and more can be received.
Breathe it all in.
Absorb it into your physical body.
The time of peace and grace for all is now.
More changes to your DNA and the way you receive, hold and carry light is at hand for all.
Be open to receiving this gift.
Go out into the world as the light you are.
Shine your light brightly.
Don't dim your light for anyone.
There are so many in need of this right now.
Trust the guidance you are receiving.
The guidance is coming from the cosmos, your spirit team and source.
Accept and trust the journey you are on.
This is all for now.

Jesus Message:

Dear Humanity: I am here at this time to remind you that the message that I spread was love... It was not to be taken out of context and it was not to be used to turn people against each other. The whole message was that we all have gifts and abilities we can all do more than we believe we can. The message was about acceptance and love not exclusion. Please now is the time when this is really important to get out there. Do not use religion or what I said to justify actions to do non-brotherly things to others. This is the time in humanity's history that we all need to come together. We are all children of God... Earth is heaven on earth, it is time to shake off the shackles and move beyond the control. Wake up to the dream within the dream. We are all divine beings. Every human has some star seed DNA as did I. We all share a lineage. The new chromosome tests are funny because that is not the DNA that needs to be tested for. Have faith humanity you do not need a leader, you all just need go unplug and go within. This is what will save humanity when you really start to see that it is one world and one race many ethnicities but one race. Then and only then will you be able to get to where you need to go.

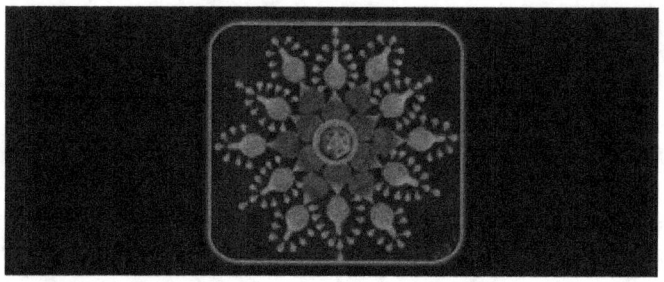

Kuan Yin Message:

I come to help humanity with being compassionate. There is so much compassion and love needed in the world right now. There has been so much destruction, loss and grief. Now is a time for all to feel held in love and to learn to pour compassion into your own lives. There are many messages and lessons from the past. The reason that I was always seen pouring is that I tried to seed humanity with compassion and self love as well as tolerance. If you do not have any of those you will turn on each other and that is exactly what happens. All come together in times of crisis however when there is no natural disaster or crisis going on all humans tend to become self-involved and lose their way. The few who think they are running the world like this, they can divide and conquer that is not what the other side wants for humanity. It is time for humanity to unite in love and compassion.

St Germain Message:

Dear Humanity:
I come to tell you about the violet flame. This flame can help with purification and burning away. It is available to all who choose to work with my energy and the flame. No special training is needed. So much that needs to be cleared from humanity's consciousness. Much hurt, pain and destruction is buried which is why it needs to be cleared, and cleansed with the violet flame so that humanity can move forward.

Mother Mary Message:

Dearest Children. . . I am always here for you sending love, peace and grace. You may call on me to help soothe fears and help when you feel over whelmed. I will send universal love, guidance and compassion in all ways. I am the mother archetype and will always come when called. I, like Kuan Yin, bring compassion and peace to help soothe the ills of humanity and each human.

Gaia Earth Mother Message:

My Children. We need to learn to live together. We are all part of this earth and we all want to survive. It is important to reacquaint yourselves with the rhythms of the earth. When you breathe I breathe. If you cover me with too much concrete and not enough trees and plants I can't breathe either. There needs to be balance and I deserve love just like each human being and animal does. We all exist together and we all need each other.

Section four:
Meditations

The Blue Flame Meditation:

First take some deep breaths in and out and center yourself. For this meditation it may be best to sit up straight in a chair. Now I want you to imagine a peaceful place for yourself it can be anywhere. Somewhere you have actually been or have always wanted to go. The only requirement is that it is a place of peace and calm. Wherever you imagine for yourself there is a bench for you to sit down on. Once you find your bench please sit down and either close your eyes or gently gaze at the images on the screen during the meditation. Whether your eyes are open or closed the energy of the images will work with you during the meditation. Take a few deep breaths in and out and let all the stress, anxiety or any racing thoughts you are having go.

Now imagine there is a blue flame above your head burning brightly. This blue flame brings a sense of peace, comfort and release when you see, feel, sense or know it. As you breathe in, the blue flame moves down into your crown chakra illuminating the whole crown chakra and gently burns away anything that is no longer needed on your journey or that is holding you back. Take a few moments and imagine the blue flame working in your crown chakra.

As you take in another deep breath, the blue flame is pulled down into your third eye chakra in the middle of your forehead. Your whole third eye chakra is illuminated with the blue flame and anything that is no longer needed on your journey or that has been holding you back is gently burned away. Take a few moments and imagine the blue flame working in your third eye chakra.

As you take in another deep breath, the blue flame is pulled down into your throat chakra. Your whole throat chakra is illuminated with the blue flame and anything that is no longer needed on your journey or that has been holding you back is gently burned away. Take a few moments and imagine the blue flame working in your throat chakra.

As you take in another deep breath, the blue flame is pulled down into your heart chakra in the middle of your chest. Your whole heart chakra is illuminated with the blue flame and anything that is no longer needed on your journey or that has been holding you back is gently burned away. Take a few moments and imagine the blue flame working in your heart chakra.

As you take in another deep breath, the blue flame is pulled down into your solar plexus or stomach chakra. Your whole solar plexus chakra is illuminated with the blue flame and anything that is no longer needed on your journey or that has been holding you back is gently burned away. Take a few moments and imagine the blue flame working in your solar plexus chakra.

As you take in another deep breath, the blue flame is pulled down into your sacral chakra halfway between your belly button and the base of your spine. Your whole sacral chakra is illuminated with the blue flame and anything that is no longer needed on your journey or that has been holding you back is gently burned away. Take a few moments and imagine the blue flame working in your sacral chakra.

As you take in another deep breath, the blue flame is pulled down into your root chakra at the base of your spine. Your whole root chakra is illuminated with the blue flame and anything that is no longer needed on your journey or that has been holding you back is gently burned away. Take a few moments and imagine the blue flame working in your root chakra.

All your chakras have now been cleaned, cleared balanced and harmonized by the blue flame. Take a few more minutes on your bench and see how you are feeling. What do you notice, is your mind clearer? Are you more focused? is your path becoming illuminated? Just sit and let whatever information you need in the moment come.

When you are ready it is time to get up from your bench and leave your peaceful place knowing that you can return any time that you need too . . .

Take a couple of breaths in and out and come back to the room where you started. Wiggle your toes and move your fingers make sure you come back fully into your physical body and enjoy.

The Healing Light Meditation:

Sit comfortably; take some deep breaths in and out. Center yourself. Please uncross arms or legs and preferably sit in a chair with feet on the floor.

Once you have centered yourself on your breath, imagine, see or feel a green, white and golden braided light over your head. Now imagine that this gold, green and white braided light comes down through your crown chakra, third eye chakra, throat chakra, heart chakra, solar plexus chakra, sacral chakra and stops at the base of your spine the root chakra. The gold, green and white braided light starts to transform and build and makes a glowing sphere in your root chakra that fills the whole chakra and base of your spine. The energy from the gold, green and white light travels down your legs and all the way into the earth. The whole bottom half of your body is saturated with this braided gold, green and white light.

The light travels up to your sacral chakra and again forms a sphere of the braided light. All the organs and structures in your body are filled with the gold, green and white braided light. As the sphere is formed in your sacral chakra all the organs and everything connected with your sacral chakra is alight with this light.

The braided gold, green and white light now travels up to your solar plexus chakra. Once in place it transforms itself into a glowing ball of braided gold, green and white light. The whole solar plexus chakra and organs are illuminated with this this light.

Now the braided light travels up to the heart chakra and again the braided gold, green and white light transforms and shifts into making a glowing sphere in your heart. The Light illuminates your chest and all organs associated with this chakra.

The braided light now travels up to your throat chakra where again it forms a glowing sphere of braided gold, green and white light. This light illuminates your throat chakra and all organs associated with this chakra.

The braided light now travels up to your third eye chakra again it transforms and shifts in a glowing braided sphere of gold, green and white light. This light illuminates your third eye and your intuition and sense of your body systems is illuminated. You can start to see how pain and dis-ease travel in your body and now have the wisdom to listen and start to heal.

The braided light now travels back up to your crown chakra. Your whole body is now illuminated with this braided gold, green and white light. The light again transforms and forms a sphere in your crown chakra.

Your whole body is now aglow with this braided gold, green and white light. All systems, nerves, bodily functions are being re aligned for optimal healing and transformation. If you want to change or transmute negative thoughts all you have to do is focus on the gold, green and white sphere in your third eye let the light heal and transform those.

If there is pain focus on the chakra associated with the pain and let the pulsating sphere of gold, green and white light heal that area.

This is to help show and teach yourself that you can listen to your body and your bodies wisdom and help to bring all systems back into alignment and harmony. This meditation is about connecting your physical body to your energy and spiritual body. To all the etheric levels. Often this is where dis-ease starts in the etheric levels and if not dealt with moves to the physical until we pay attention.

Take a few moments and see your whole spinal column aglow and trying to reconfigure itself into the healthiest version it can be in.

It is time we all awaken to the gift of us all being our own healers and challenging our own thoughts and limiting beliefs.
Namaste

The Golden Christos Light Meditation:

Take a couple of deep breaths and center yourself.   Focus on your breath going in and out. Lie or sit comfortably. The more relaxed and centered you become you notice that there is a sphere of glowing golden Christos light in front of you. The more you connect with this sphere of glowing golden light the more relaxed and peaceful you become.

This sphere of golden light is placed into your heart chakra, as it is placed there you feel an immense love and sense of gratitude. You feel a sudden sense of peace and calm. The golden sphere of light in your heart chakra starts to expand and first goes down your torso and all the way down both legs illuminating the lower half of your body with this golden light. The golden lights shoots out the bottom of your feet and goes all the way down into the earth and is anchored in the earth.

Now the golden light moves up the top half of body and down your arms until the entire top half of your body is glowing in golden light. The golden light shoots out your crown chakra like a cascading waterfall and fills all of your subtle bodies with this golden light.

This golden light heals, clears and aligns you with the pure Christos energy of the earth and of the cosmos. You are now fully connected above and below.

How does this feel? Notice any sensations that come up in your body?

Epilogue

I would like to thank all of you who have taken the time to read the words that have been written, to allow yourself to go on this journey. Mostly to be open to living the life you are meant to be living and to stop comparing yourself with others.

If there is one thing that I may be so bold to leave you with: You are enough. That is all. You are enough. You matter, you have value. We are called human beings for a reason. Being is enough and you are enough. Sometimes something that may seem so simple is so very difficult.

I wish you a good journey fellow traveler. That is what we are travelers and we all have a path and a journey. It is always amazing when we cross paths. We will cross again because we are all connected and are all one.

Namaste!

www.ingramcontent.com/pod-product-compliance
Lightning Source LLC
Chambersburg PA
CBHW051407290426
44108CB00015B/2189